DISCOVER EARTH'S SECRETS

Editor: STEVE PARKER

DAVID AND HELEN ORME

QED Publishing

Designer and Picture Researcher Louise Downey
Project Editor Michael Downey

Copyright © QED Publishing 2011

First published in the UK in 2011 by
QED Publishing
A Quarto Group company
230 City Road
London EC1V 2TT

www.qed-publishing.co.uk

A catalogue record for this book is
available from the British Library.

ISBN 978 1 84835 696 2

Printed in China

Picture Credits

Key: t=top, b=bottom, c=centre,
FC=front cover
Corbis 13t Colin Garratt; Milepost 921/4/ 16-17 Julie
Dermansky/ 29t Patrick Pleul-dpa/ 40b G.J. McCarthy/Dallas
Morning News/ 46b Bryn Colton/46-47 Nic Bothma/epa /
Assignments Photographers/ 54-55 Guenter Rossenbach/ 58-59
Diego Azubel/epa/ 81c Bettmann/ 82-83 Anatoly Maltsev-epa/
83c Menno Boermans-Aurora Photos/ 84b Jeremy Horner / 85t
STR-epa/ 98-99 Mike Hollingshead/Science Faction/ 99t epa/
100-101t George Steinmetz/ 100-101b epa/ 101t Chris Mattison;
Frank Lane Picture Agency/ 106 Visuals Unlimited/ 110-111
Dorling Kindersley 105t
Getty Images 14-15 Philip and Karen Smith/ 36b Joseph
Van Os/ 38 Stephen Alvarez/ 42-43t Kreg Holt/ 43c Phillippe
Bourseiller/ 45t National Geographic/ 50 Kim Westerskov/
53b Time & Life Pictures/ 56-57t Panoramic Images/ 57b/
68b Paul Chesley/ 69b Dario Mitidieri-Contributor / 71t /72
Arctic-Images/ 72b Travel Pix/ 92-93/ 112 STasker/ 113b Sakis
Papadopoulos/
Louise Downey 17t/ 94t/ 97b/
Michael Penn / NYT / Redux / eyevine 45b/
NASA 6b ESA, J. Hester, A. Loll (ASU)/ 9t/ 31, 32, 33/ 60, 61, 62/
76br NASA/USGS/Tammy Becker and Paul Geissler / 704t/
Photoshot 20 NHPA/ 21b Woodfall Wild Images/ 23 World
Pictures/ 26 NHPA/ 27 Xinhua/ 28t Xinhua/ 31 NHPA/ 48/ 49
AllCanadaPhotos/ 55t/ 76-77 VWPics/113 Imagebrokers/

Science Photo Library 6-7 Mark Garlick/
9 Mark Garlick/ 10t SPL/ 10b Lynette Cook/ 13b Patrick
Landmann/ 14b Gary Hincks/ 16b Karim Agabi / Eurellios/
20b Gary Hincks/ 22b Gary Hinks/ 24b Javier Trueba / MSF/
28b Gary Hincks/
Science Photo Library 39t Daniel Sambraus/ 51 W. Haxby,
Lamont-Doherty Earth observatory/ 52b Jacques Jangoux/
64-65 Gary Hincks/64t Gary Hincks/ 67t Mikkel Juul
Jensen-Bonnier Publications/ 66c Christian Darkin/ 74–75
Prof. Stewart Lowther/ 78t Dr Ken MacDonald/ 78b Dr Ken
MacDonald/ 79 Dr Ken MacDonald/ 80b Gary Hincks/ 84-
85 Gary Hincks/ 97 Pekka Parviainen/ 99b Gary Hincks/
103b Lino Pastorelli/ 106t Gary Hincks/ 112b Gary Hincks/
Shutterstock 3/ 4-5/ 32-33/ 34 Chris Hill/ 7b Linda Brotkorb/
8 sdecoret/ 11t Galyna Andrushko/ 12 argonaut/ 18 Nikki
Bidgood / 19b Jose Gil/ 19 Vulkanette/ 21t Beschi/ 23c Elena
Elisseeva/ 24-25t Dmitri Melnik/ 24c Don Bendickson/ 25b Jiri
Vaclavek/ 27t Geowulf/ 28-29 Tonylady/ 30 Pichugin Dmitry/
31b William Allum/ 34-35 szefei/ 35t nikolpetr/ 35b/
36-37 K. Kolygo/ 37t George Burba/ 37b Roger De Marfa/ 39
Sally Scott/ 40t Stephanie Coffman/ 40c Boykov/ 40-41 Imagine
Images Alastair Pidgen/ 41t Xavier Marchant/ 41b Pavelk/
42-43b Sam D Cruz/ 44-45 marchello/ 44b mountainpix/
47t Gertjan Hooijer/ 47b Atlaspix/ 49t bierchen/ 51b Donald
Gargano/ 52-53 Elisabeth Holm/ 53t Perkoptimal/ 54b
Michael Shake/ 55b Vinicius Tupinamba/ 57t Thor Jorgen
Udvang/ 56-57b Martin D. Vonka/ 58b agophoto/59t steve
estvanik/ 59l Andrejs Pidjass/ 59tr Eric Gevaert/ 62b Shipov
Oleg/ 62-63 Jon Naustdalslid/ 64Lysithee/ 67c Map Resources/
markrhiggins/ 68-69 Supertrooper/ 70-71 Volodymyr Goinyk/
70b iNNOCENt/ 71 Caitlin Mirra/ 73 Gian Corrêa Saléro/
75b John Hua/ 76b gracious_tiger/ 77t Supertrooper/ 82t
Juha Sompinmäki/ 86c Andreas Meyer/ 86 JCElv/ 87 Walter
G Arce/ 88-89/ 116-117/ 118 2009fotofriends/ 90-91 Scott
Prokop/ 90b Paolo Albertosi/ 91c WORAKIT/ 93b Tiberiu
Stan/ 93t Supertrooper/ 94-95 Tyler Olson/ 94b Dark o/ 96
basel101658/ 96t majeczka/ 96c Jozsef Szasz-Fabian/ 96b Paul
Aniszewski/ 99c Pavel Cheiko/ 102-103 James "BO" Insogna/
104-105 Ramon Berk/ 105 Caitlin Mirra/ 107 jam4travel/
108-109 ArchMan/ 109b Stephen Finn/ 110 Lisa F. Young/
111b parnick/ 111t kesipun/ 114-115 T.W. van Urk/ 115 I.
Quintanilla/

Words in **bold** are
explained in the
Glossary on page 116.

Contents

Tell me more!

These fossilized shells were once
Ammonites. Ammonites were molluscs.
Other molluscs include snails, clams,
squid, octopus and cuttlefish. Like squid,
Ammonites could move backwards by
shooting out water from their bodies.

In the beginning

To know what is inside the Earth, we need to look back at where our planet came from. Its story started 4600 million years ago.

Gas cloud

The star we call the Sun, and all the objects going around it, are together called the Solar System. These objects include the Earth and seven other planets, their moons and countless smaller lumps of rock. They all began as a vast cloud of gas and dust spinning in space.

The Sun and planets gradually formed from a giant whirling cloud in space.

Tell me more!

The dust and gas that became our Solar System probably formed when a huge, old star blew apart in an explosion called a **supernova**. Everything in the Solar System, therefore, is made of stardust – the Sun, the planets and their moons, and even us!

Sun and planets

As the cloud whirled around, small amounts of gas and dust began to clump together. This happened because of the pulling power that all matter has, called **gravity**. Some clumps slowly became bigger and heavier. The largest, in the centre, formed the Sun and started to shine. Smaller clumps became the planets.

Sun

Mercury

Earth

Venus

Jupiter

Mars

Saturn

Uranus

Neptune

Earth is the fifth biggest of the eight planets, and third out from the Sun in our Solar System.

Early Earth

As gas and dust clumped together to form the Earth, they became extremely hot. Gradually, our planet took shape as a spinning ball.

Massive bang

Early in its history, it is possible that the Earth was hit by another, smaller planet. This collision may have knocked a chunk out of the Earth, which became the Moon. The collision may also have tilted the Earth, which does not spin upright, but slightly to one side.

A smaller planet may have crashed into the Earth not long after it formed.

Red-hot world

Slowly, parts of the Earth's surface began to harden into solid rock. Other parts of the surface remained as red-hot liquid rock. Huge volcanoes spurted out poison gases in many places. There was no life for a billion years.

The surface of the early Earth was made up of boiling rocks and huge volcanoes.

Bringing water

During our Solar System's early history, there were millions of lumps of rock and ice hurtling around in space. Thousands of these smashed into the Earth. Some of these, called **comets**, may have brought water to Earth as it cooled.

Layered Earth

The Earth is made up of layers. These start with
the inner core at the centre and end with the crust.

Earth's crust

The outer layer of the Earth
is known as the **crust**. This
is the layer we live on. In
some places, such as at the
bottom of the sea, the crust
is only 5 kilometres thick.
In other places, especially
under mountains, the
crust can be up to
60 kilometres thick.

Jagged edges

The Earth's crust is not
one solid piece. It is more
like a cracked eggshell
around an egg. The
crust is made of huge,
curved pieces that have
jagged edges. These
fit together like the
pieces of a gigantic
jigsaw puzzle.

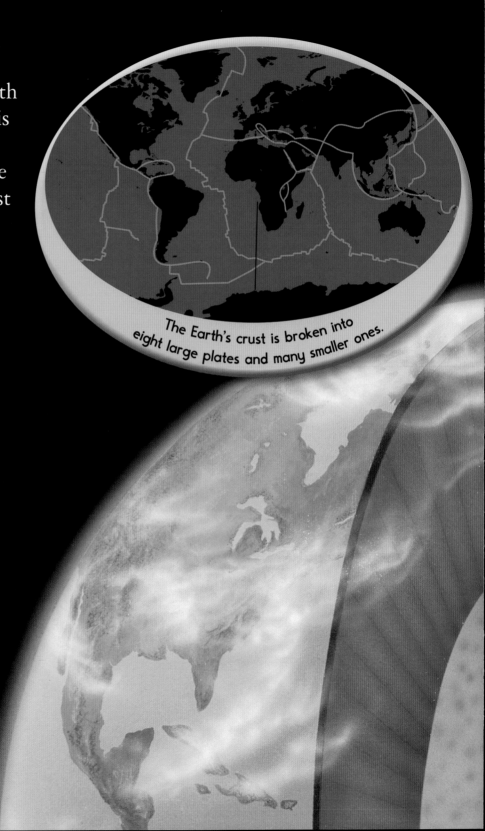

The Earth's crust is broken into
eight large plates and many smaller ones.

Hot mantle

Under the crust is a much thicker layer called the **mantle**. This is about 2900 kilometres deep. The rocks here are extremely hot and partly molten, or melted. They move and flow like thick jelly. The crust's plates slide around slowly on the soft mantle.

Where rocks are worn away, such as in the Grand Canyon, we can see deeper into the crust.

Inner core

At the centre of the Earth is the core. This is made up mostly of the metals iron and nickel. Although the outer core is molten, the inner core is solid and very hot!

The Earth's four main layers are the crust, the mantle, the outer core and the inner core.

Crust

Mantle

Outer core

Inner core

Tell me more!

The Earth's crust seems huge, thick and solid. But if the whole planet were shrunk down to the size of an apple, the crust would be thinner and weaker than the skin of a real apple!

The Earth has been around for more than 4000 million years. Its crust is cool but its middle, or core, is still extremely hot. Can we work out how hot?

Hotter than the Sun

It is not possible for scientists to drill down to the inner core to measure how hot it is. Instead, they have to make complicated calculations. Scientists believe that at the centre of the Earth the temperature may be as high as 7000 degrees Celsius. This is hotter than the surface of the Sun!

The deepest that people have drilled into the crust is about 12 kilometres. This is less than one-third of the way through the crust.

Staying hot

Part of the heat that comes from the Earth's core is heat left over from when the Earth was first formed. Heat is also created in the core by **radioactive substances**. These give off large amounts of heat as they slowly break down into simpler substances. This is what happens in a nuclear power station. The radioactive fuel gives off heat, which is then used to generate electricity.

Tell me more!

How deep into the Earth can people go? There are gold mines in South Africa that are nearly 4 kilometres deep. Some of these mines are fitted with special equipment that keeps miners cool. Underground temperatures can reach a blistering 70 degrees Celsius!

Workers change the radioactive fuel in a power station.

Earth's magnetism

Deep inside the Earth, the core is slowly moving and flowing in circles. How do we know this happens? We know this because of the magnetic **compass**!

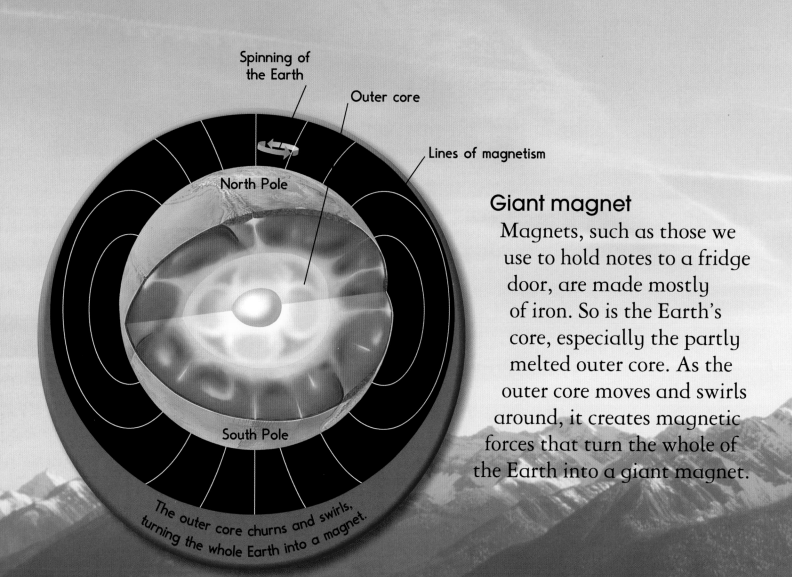

Spinning of the Earth

Outer core

Lines of magnetism

North Pole

South Pole

The outer core churns and swirls, turning the whole Earth into a magnet.

Giant magnet

Magnets, such as those we use to hold notes to a fridge door, are made mostly of iron. So is the Earth's core, especially the partly melted outer core. As the outer core moves and swirls around, it creates magnetic forces that turn the whole of the Earth into a giant magnet.

How a compass works

A compass needle is a long, thin magnet. When it can turn freely, it lines up with the magnetism of the whole Earth. The ends of the compass needle point to the places where Earth's magnetism is strongest – the North Pole at the top of the planet, and the South Pole at the bottom.

People can discover which way is north by using a compass.

Tell me more!

Every few million years, the Earth's magnetism reverses, or flips. The North Pole becomes the South Pole, and the other way around. In a few thousand years, this may happen again. Then, a compass needle's north end will point south!

15

The mantle

The mantle forms more than four-fifths
of the whole Earth. It is so hot that
some of its rocks are melted or molten.

During an earthquake,
the ground can shake
and move so much that
buildings collapse. This
happened in Haiti in 2010.

Moving mantle

The outer part of the mantle, at the bottom
of the crust, has a temperature of about 500
degrees Celsius. The inner mantle, which is next
to the core, is more than 4000 degrees Celsius.
Rocks in the mantle slowly flow up,
sideways and down again.

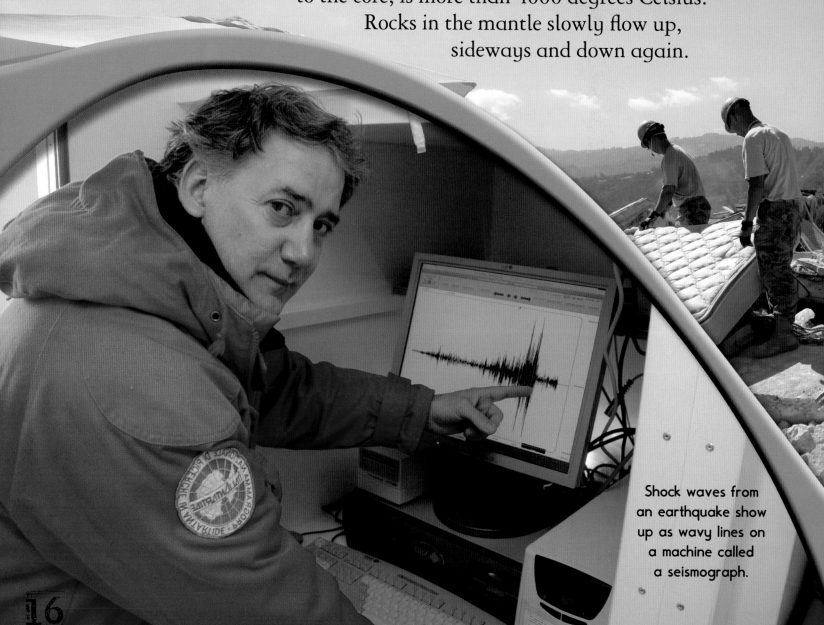

Shock waves from
an earthquake show
up as wavy lines on
a machine called
a seismograph.

Shock waves

An earthquake is the sudden jolting of the enormous crust **plates** as they rub past each other. This jolting sends out shock waves, also called seismic waves. Some waves travel through the crust. Others pass into the Earth and are bent by the mantle and core to reach the Earth's surface far away. The speed and extent of bending show us what the mantle is made of.

Crust

Mantle

Outer core

Inner core

Earthquake

Seismic waves bend as they pass through the Earth's mantle and core.

Tell me more!

Seismic waves, which travel between one and 15 kilometres per second, may take more than an hour to reach the opposite side of the world. By that time they are weak and only a seismograph can detect them.

Rocky crust

The rocks that form our planet are made in different ways.

Soft rocks have been worn away by wind and rain to leave these hard granite rocks.

Rock types

There are three basic rock types. These are the **igneous**, **sedimentary** and **metamorphic** rocks. Igneous rocks form when extremely hot and runny lava or magma cool down and become solid.

Tell me more!

The world's biggest single rock, 350 metres high and 9.5 kilometres around, is Uluru in Central Australia. It is made of the sedimentary rock sandstone.

Magma rocks

The molten rock deep in the Earth's crust and mantle is called **magma**. This runny rock can rise up nearer to the surface, cool and then harden into an igneous rock, such as granite. These rocks are seen when the surface of the Earth is worn away by wind and rain to uncover deeper layers.

Lava rocks

Magma can also rise up to the surface through a weak part in the Earth's crust. When this happens in volcanoes, the magma is called **lava**. The lava flows out, cools and hardens into igneous rocks of different shapes and patterns.

Red-hot lava oozes slowly from some volcanoes, and spurts out with a fiery explosion from others.

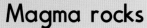

This lava has cooled into long, sausage-like shapes known as pahoehoe, or ropy lava.

Layers of rock

Sedimentary rocks are made from millions
and millions of tiny pieces, or particles,
which have been squeezed together.

Squashed into rock

Over millions of years, wind, rain, rivers and ice wear
away parts of the Earth into tiny pieces, such as sand,
mud and silt. These get washed into rivers and are carried
out to sea, where they sink to the bottom in layers known
as sediments. As the layers pile up, the lowest ones are
squashed into rocks, such as sandstone and limestone.

Sedimentary layers
on the seabed

Earth's movements
break the layers

Layers of particles on the seabed are
pressed into sedimentary rocks.

The Painted Hills in
Oregon, United States,
were once silt, clay and
mud left when a river
flooded the land.

Changing rocks

Once rocks are formed they can be changed in many ways. Massive movement of the Earth can push them up into mountains. These movements may also press rocks down into the magma. Heat and pressure in deep layers can 'cook' igneous and sedimentary rock types, changing them into rocks called metamorphic rocks. Marble is a metamorphic rock.

Tell me more!

Rocks from seabed sediments, such as chalk and limestone, often contain the remains of plants and animals. These are called **fossils**. Some types of chalk are mostly made up of fossils!

In millions of years, these mud banks by the River Ganges in India may become hard rock.

Caves

Rainwater that seeps deep into the cracks in rocks sometimes creates amazing cave systems.

Cracks and shafts

After it rains, water seeps into the ground through the soil. This rainwater will gradually sink deeper and deeper through cracks in the rock. Sometimes, streams and even small rivers can disappear through vertical shafts called **sinkholes**. The water may reappear again many miles away.

Stalactites form very slowly, drip by drip. They sometimes get so heavy they break off.

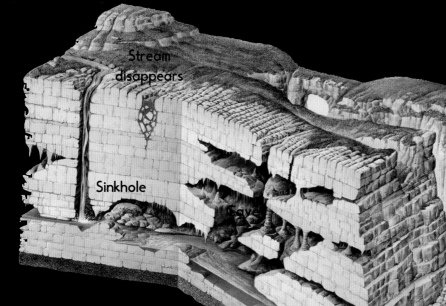

Stream disappears

Sinkhole

Cave

Spring

A stream eats away tunnels and caves in a limestone hill and reappears lower down the slope.

Stalagmites 'grow' about two centimetres every 100 years.

Limestone caves

Most caves form in limestone rock. This is because limestone is slowly eaten away, or dissolved, by rainwater. At first the caves are full of water. As more limestone dissolves, the caves deepen and the higher parts become dry. Water dripping from the roof leaves behind particles of limestone that form icicle-shaped stalactites. Where it drips onto the floor, it can build upside-down versions known as stalagmites.

Earth minerals

Rocks are made of substances called minerals. Some of these are very precious and beautiful.

Rare and precious

Minerals form deep in the Earth over long periods of time. Some, such as gypsum, calcite and various kinds of salt, are very common. Others, such as diamonds and gold, are rare and precious. Some rocks are also valuable. These include granite and marble, which are used in buildings.

Pure gold is sometimes found in streams.

Mexico's Cave of Crystals contains amazingly shaped crystals, some more than 10 metres long.

Digging mines

To take rocks and minerals from the Earth, we dig mines. In a deep-shaft mine, sideways tunnels are made at the bottom of a deep hole. Open-cast mines and quarries, or giant pits, are created near the surface. Rocks and minerals are removed from these by using huge excavator machines and explosives.

Dynamite breaks apart rocks in an open-cast mine.

Amethyst is a form of the mineral quartz.

Tell me more!

Diamonds are made of **carbon** and can take billions of years to form. They are created deep inside the Earth under great heat and pressure. Diamonds only find their way to the Earth's surface when they are carried up by the flow of magma.

Fossils

When animals and plants die, their bodies usually rot away. After a few years, there is nothing left. In some cases, however, **traces** of their hard parts remain.

How fossils form

Fossils are found in sedimentary rocks. They are both the preserved hard parts of animals, such as bones, teeth and shells, and the impression or shape of animals left in the mud. Many fossils of the hard parts of plants, such as the bark and seeds, have also been found. The parts are buried in sediments and, like the sediments, they gradually turn into solid rock over millions of years.

Tell me more!

In 2009, fossil hunters in France found the world's biggest dinosaur footprints — each one was about 1.5 metres across! These footprints were probably made by a 30-tonne **sauropod** about 150 million years ago.

Fossils enable scientists to reconstruct the skeletons of ancient creatures.

Fossil record

Fossils tell us about the kinds of animals and plants that lived in the past. This is called the fossil record. It shows how life changed, or evolved, over millions of years. Knowing how fast the layers of sedimentary rocks were laid down allows us to work out the age of the fossils.

Curly-shelled ammonites are common fossils.

These fossil bones have been put back together to make the skeletons of a huge plant-eating dinosaur and two smaller meat-eaters.

Fossil fuels

The coal, oil and **natural gas** that we use today are known as fossil fuels. They were made millions of years ago from dead plants and animals.

Vast amounts of coal are dug from the earth.

Coal from plants

Hundreds of millions of years ago, giant plants grew in **swamps**. As the plants died, they fell into the water, forming layers. The plants did not rot very fast, and they piled up deeper. Gradually, they were covered by sediments and squashed, forming the black rock called coal.

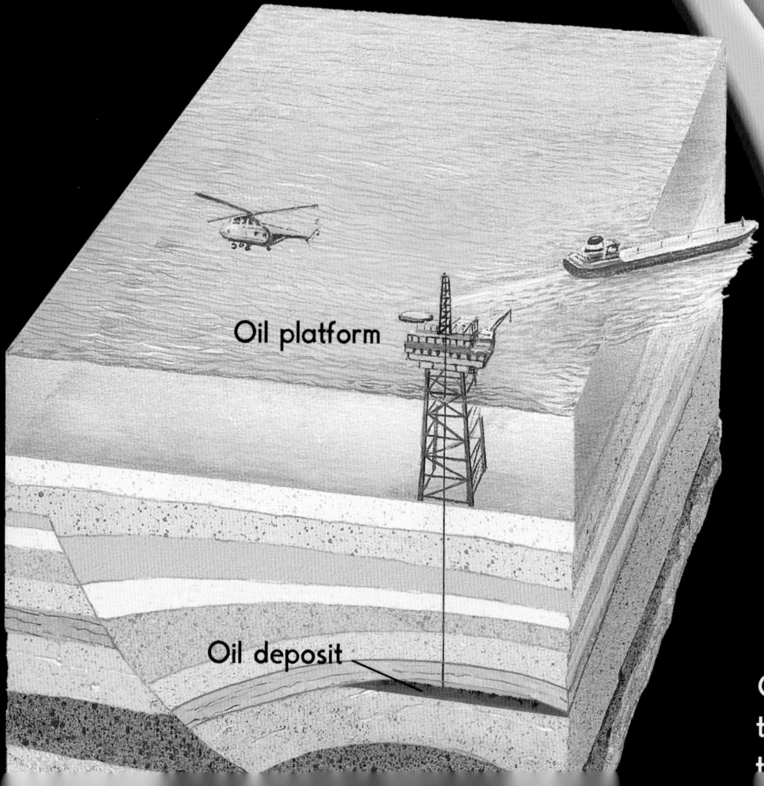

Oil platform

Oil deposit

Oil rigs drill through the seabed to reach trapped oil and gas.

Oil and natural gas

A long time ago, tiny animals and plants called **plankton** lived in the seas – just as they do today. As they died, they sank and settled in the mud. This muddy layer was then slowly covered over, compressed and became hot. This process turned the squashed material into oil and natural gas. When trapped by a layer of hard rock above, the oil and gas collected, ready to be discovered millions of years later.

Oil platforms guide oil or gas along undersea pipelines, or load it into giant tanker ships.

Tell me more!

Digging coal out of the ground can be very hard work. But not for the world's biggest digging machine! Trencher 2 is the length of two-and-a-half football pitches end to end!

Hot Earth

In some places around the world, hot rocks are found near the surface. We can use their heat to make electricity and to warm ourselves and our homes.

Hot geysers

Heat from the Earth is known as geothermal energy. In some places, such as New Zealand, you can touch the rocks and feel their warmth. Water trickling through deep cracks in the rocks may burst out as a shower of steam and boiling water. This is known as a **geyser**.

The Pohutu Geyser in New Zealand sprays out scalding water and steam up to 100 metres into the air every 30 minutes.

Once a geothermal power station is built, like this one in Iceland, it costs very little to run. Also, it does not produce greenhouse gases or other forms of pollution.

Tell me more!

In most places, the rocks of the crust get hotter by 3 degrees Celsius for every 100 metres you go down. But in geyser areas, the rocks are more than 200 degrees Celsius just a few tens of metres down!

Geothermal electricity

To make geothermal electricity, holes for pipes are drilled deep into hot rocks. Cold water is then pumped down through one set of pipes and comes up through another set very hot. The heat can be used to generate electricity in a geothermal power station.

Hot springs are popular with Japanese macaque monkeys, who relax in the warm water.

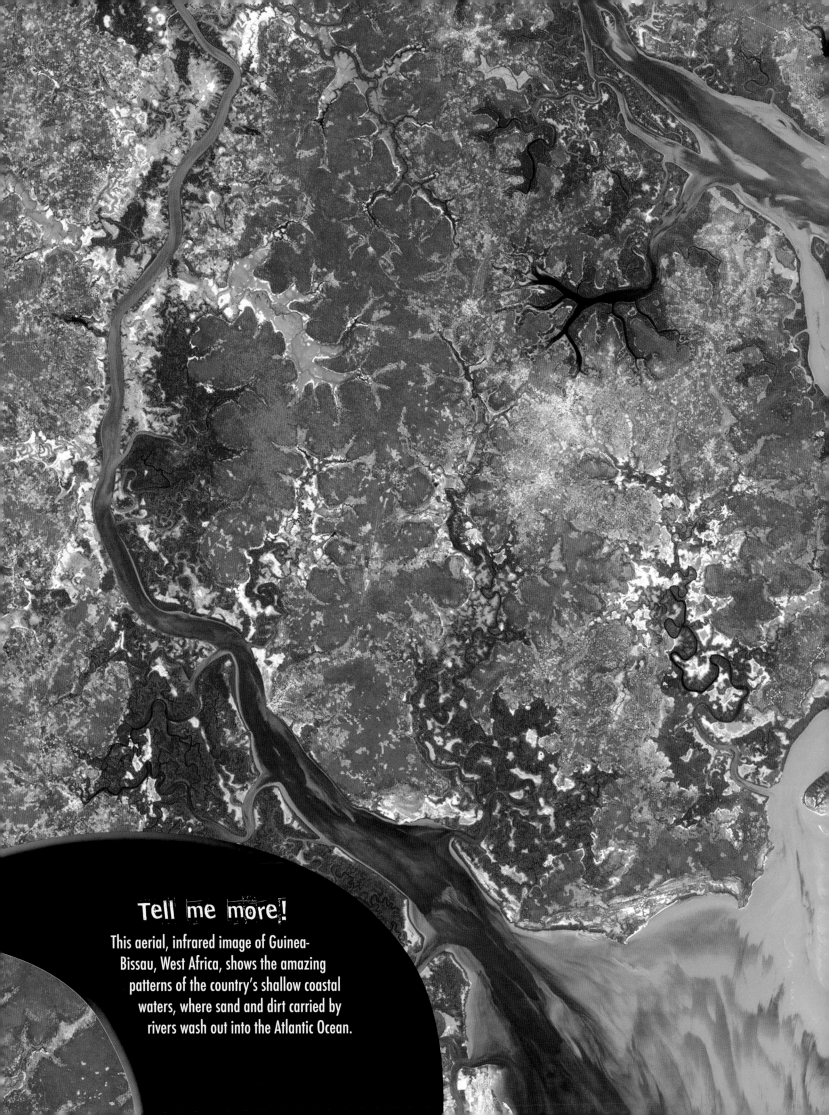

Tell me more!

This aerial, infrared image of Guinea-Bissau, West Africa, shows the amazing patterns of the country's shallow coastal waters, where sand and dirt carried by rivers wash out into the Atlantic Ocean.

What shapes the Earth?

The Earth's surface is always changing. Strong winds, heavy rain, freezing ice, fierce storms, and rushing floods alter the land. Our coasts are changed by waves, ocean currents, and unstoppable tides.

Ice and water

Freezing and melting ice can crack rocks. Huge **glaciers** of ice carve deep valleys, and rivers move rocks and soil from one place to another.

Volcanoes erupt and build new peaks, such as in the Tengger mountains in Java, Indonesia.

New York City in the United States stands on land that was once thick with forests.

Mighty forces

Many changes that shape the Earth are very slow. But others are sudden and violent such as powerful earthquakes and erupting volcanoes.

Tell me more!

A big sandstorm can move giant sand dunes many miles. Sometimes, sand is blown away from one place, leaving behind bare rocks. This sand may then fill up a valley somewhere else.

Human impact

People are altering the Earth in many ways. We build cities with tall buildings, cut down forests and change the way rivers flow. We drain wetlands and push back the sea to make fields for crops. Today, huge areas of land are being shaped by us.

Building up

Huge mountains have risen up in many parts of the world. Most of these mountains formed over millions of years, but some islands have formed in just one day.

Earth's plates

The Earth's hard outer layer of rock, the crust, is not one solid shell of rock. It is more like a cracked egg made up of giant, curved plates of rock. These jagged plates, move slowly over millions of years. When two plates push together, their edges bend and crumple to form tall, sharp-topped mountains.

When two of the Earth's plates move apart, they leave a huge crack in the surface, such as the Great Rift Valley in East Africa.

Exploding volcanoes

In some places the Earth's rocky crust is much thinner. Red-hot liquid rock lies just below this thin crust. Sometimes, this liquid rock builds up so much pressure that it pushes through the crust to form a volcano. The runny rock, called lava, may ooze out slowly or burst out as an eruption.

Hot liquid rock from volcanoes cools at the surface and goes hard.

When two of the Earth's surface plates rub against each other, rocks crack and bend up to form mountains, such as the Alps in Europe.

Tell me more!

The remains of sea animals are found high on mountains! Rocks that were once the seabed have been pushed up into mountains, complete with creatures from long ago that are now fossils.

37

Wearing down

The Earth's surface is shaped by the forces of wind, rain, frost and ice. These slowly wear away the land. This process is called erosion.

Erosion underground

Rainwater trickles down through cracks in rocks, slowly working its way deeper and deeper. The steady trickle **dissolves** some stones, such as limestone, making small cracks larger. This type of erosion eats away rocks under the surface to form huge caves and caverns – some as large as cities!

The world's largest caves, such as the Mammoth Caves in Kentucky, USA, were made by rainwater erosion.

Tell me more!

In the 1930s, the Great Plains of Canada and the United States suffered severe wind erosion due to drought and bad farming methods. Much of the rich soil blew away in great dust storms.

Power of ice

When water trickles into cracks in rocks and freezes into ice, it spreads out, or expands. This **expansion** forces open the cracks, making them wider. Slowly, over months and years, bits of rock break off and split into smaller pieces. This type of erosion happens underground as well as on the Earth's surface.

This broken rock has been split by water freezing into ice.

Erosion by wind

A gentle breeze can pick up dust and blow it against rocks. Over thousands of years, this dusty breeze can wear away even the hardest rock. Strong winds hurl around larger bits, such as sand and gravel, which can erode rocks into strange shapes.

Wind has sandblasted and eroded these rocks near Colorado Springs in the United States.

Rivers

Rivers flow from high to low ground. On their journey, they erode hills and mountains, sometimes cutting deep **gorges**. Rivers also carry water to dry places, allowing plants to grow.

Rainwater creates mountain streams and waterfalls.

In the mountains

Rivers start out in hills and mountains. Water flows down slopes in small streams, which join together to form larger streams and then rivers. As a river nears the coast, it crosses areas of flatter land and flows more slowly. Sand, mud and other bits settle along its bed and banks. Heavy rain can flood these flat areas, which are known as **flood plains**.

Rivers are powerful enough to cut deep mountain gorges.

Heavy rain can bring masses of water into flood plains.

Out to sea

When the river reaches the sea, it deposits more material. Often, the river spreads out into many channels, forming a **delta**. After this, any material still being carried by the water flows out to sea. Over millions of years, this material builds up on the seabed.

Lack of water

If not enough rain falls, rivers can dry up and even disappear. If people take out too much water, rivers may also shrink and turn into dry, cracked channels.

Tell me more!

Over many millions of years, the Colorado River in the USA has cut a deep channel through the rocks. This created a famous gorge called the Grand Canyon. In parts, it is more than 1800 metres deep!

At 6690 kilometres, the River Nile in Egypt is the world's longest river.

River deltas are made up of many smaller channels.

Ice rivers

Northern Europe

North America

The white areas show how much land and sea were covered by ice 20,000 years ago.

During the last **Ice Age**, much of the Earth was covered by ice sheets and glaciers. Today, glaciers are found only in the coldest regions.

Changing landscape

About 20,000 years ago, during the last Ice Age, parts of North America and Northern Europe were covered with ice. This ice began to melt 10,000 years ago when the world warmed up. Today, although much of the ice has gone, we can still see how it changed the landscape.

Ice is lighter than water, so glaciers and ice sheets float on the sea.

Huge valleys

The biggest changes to the landscape were made by massive 'rivers' of ice called glaciers. These formed high up a mountain where it was too cold for snow to melt. Falling snow piled up higher and higher, pressing on the snow beneath to form hard-packed ice. This ice then moved slowly down the mountain, carving out a huge valley. Today, glaciers are found only in the highest mountains and in the **polar regions**, where it is freezing all year around.

Tell me more!

Under a glacier, melting water can erode rock to form glacier caves. These are exciting and beautiful, but dangerous to explore!

Floating ice is a danger to boats in Glacier Bay, Alaska, USA.

Massive icebergs

Most glaciers melt as they slide down mountains to where it is warmer. Some glaciers, however, are still frozen when they reach the sea. Huge chunks of ice can break off these glaciers and float away as icebergs. The biggest icebergs can be hundreds of kilometres wide!

Glacier power

Glaciers carve out deep valleys and move large amounts of rock and other material from one place to another. These features can be seen where the glaciers have long disappeared.

This U-shaped valley was carved out by a glacier.

Lysefjord in southern Norway is 40 kilometres long. It was formed during the last Ice Age.

Flooded valleys

When a valley that has been made by glaciers runs into the sea, it may be flooded by sea water. This type of flooded river valley is known as a **fjord**. Many fjords are found in some northern European countries, particularly on the coast of Norway. During the last Ice Age, Norway was entirely covered in ice.

Tell me more!

Glacier ice is made from snow that fell over thousands of years. It may contain wind-blown seeds and even tiny animals. Scientists study this ice to find out about the world's climate and life that existed long ago.

Rising land

During the last Ice Age, the huge weight of ice pushed down the land. As the climate became warmer and the ice melted, the ground started to move up again. This movement is still happening today. In Glacier Bay, Alaska, so many large glaciers have melted over thousands of years that the land still rises by eight centimetres a year.

This dry land in Alaska's Glacier Bay was under water 20 years ago.

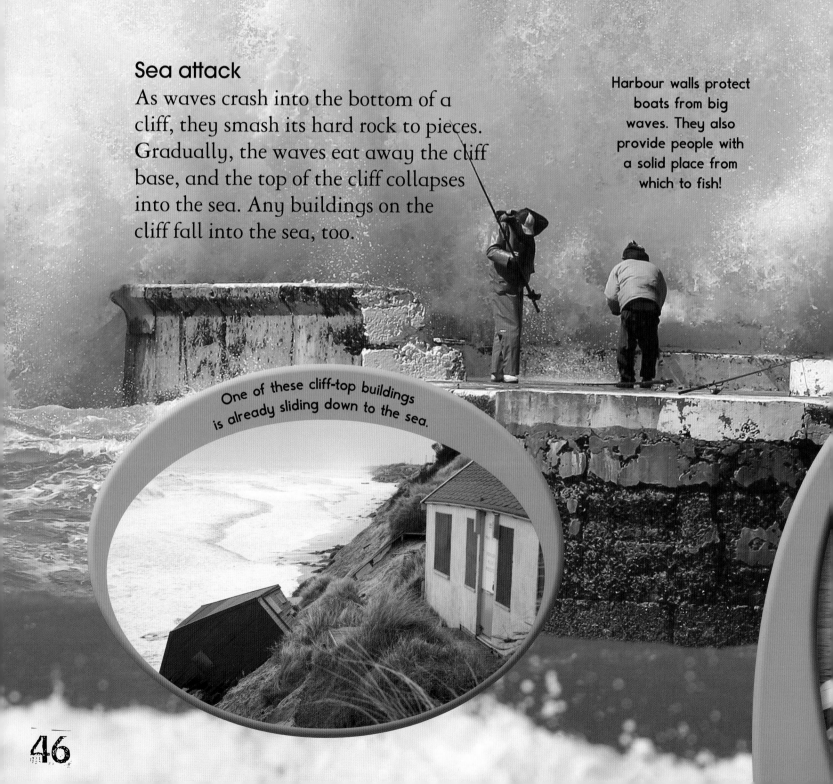

Coastal areas

Day and night, the Earth's coasts and shores are battered by the sea. Strong sea walls can help to protect some coastal areas from the worst effects of this coastal erosion.

Sea attack

As waves crash into the bottom of a cliff, they smash its hard rock to pieces. Gradually, the waves eat away the cliff base, and the top of the cliff collapses into the sea. Any buildings on the cliff fall into the sea, too.

Harbour walls protect boats from big waves. They also provide people with a solid place from which to fish!

One of these cliff-top buildings is already sliding down to the sea.

New land

Along the coast, waves and currents roll and break big rocks into smaller pieces, such as shingle, sand and mud. These are carried by tides and currents along the coast to make sandy beaches, sand dunes and mud flats. Over a long period of time, these areas build up into new land.

Tell me more!

This land at Eemnes, the Netherlands, was once under the sea! It has been reclaimed by the building of sea walls and by digging channels to drain away water.

These concrete blocks and the reinforced wall protect the coastline.

Tidal times

A tide is the daily rise and fall of water in a sea or in an ocean. As it goes up and down, water wears away seaside sand and rocks, and shapes the shore.

At high tide, waves wear away high parts of the shore, including this harbour wall.

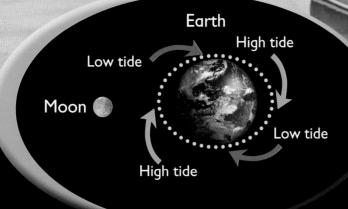

Earth

High tide

Low tide

Moon

Low tide

High tide

The large yellow dots show the bulges in the oceans caused by the Moon's gravity. The red arrows show places with low tides, the green ones show high tides.

High and low

The Moon's gravity makes the ocean nearest to it bulge towards it. This is high tide. At the same time, there is another bulge of water on the opposite side of the Earth. Between these two high tides, there is a low tide. As the Earth spins around each day, the bulges move around its surface

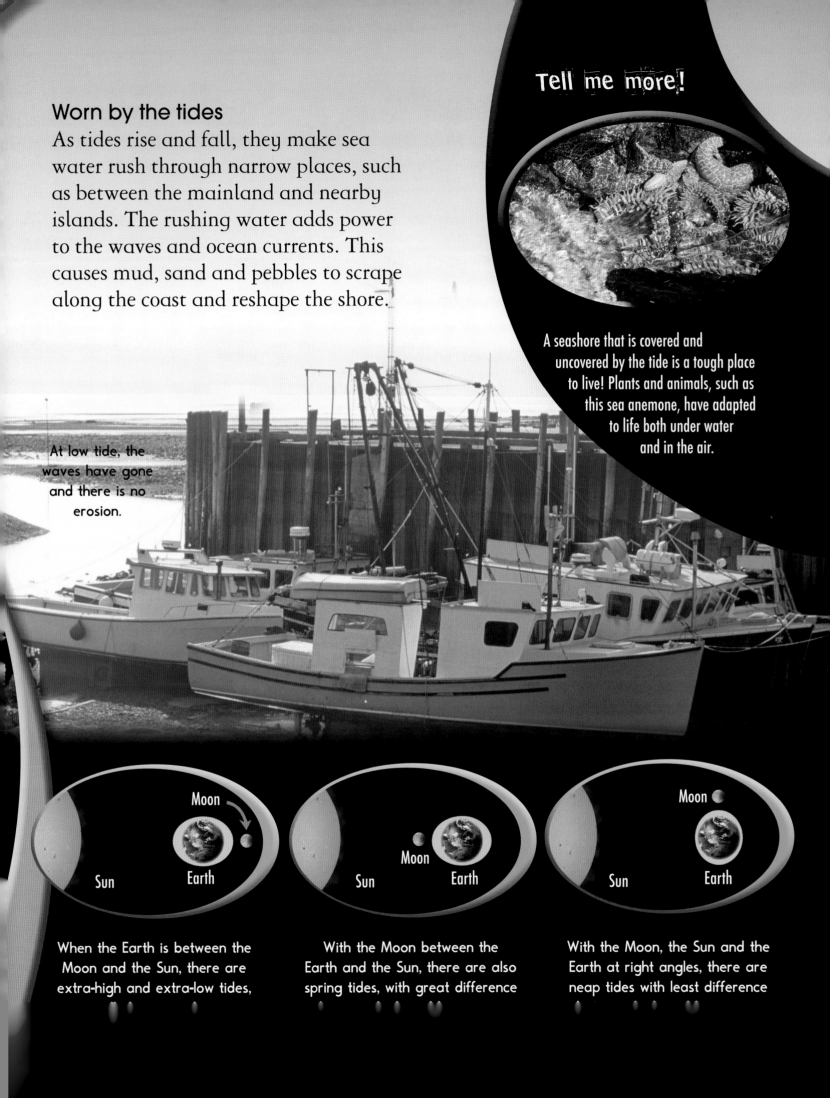

Worn by the tides

As tides rise and fall, they make sea water rush through narrow places, such as between the mainland and nearby islands. The rushing water adds power to the waves and ocean currents. This causes mud, sand and pebbles to scrape along the coast and reshape the shore.

At low tide, the waves have gone and there is no erosion.

Tell me more!

A seashore that is covered and uncovered by the tide is a tough place to live! Plants and animals, such as this sea anemone, have adapted to life both under water and in the air.

Moon

Sun   Earth

Moon

Sun   Earth

Moon

Sun   Earth

When the Earth is between the Moon and the Sun, there are extra-high and extra-low tides,

With the Moon between the Earth and the Sun, there are also spring tides, with great difference

With the Moon, the Sun and the Earth at right angles, there are neap tides with least difference

Shaping the seabed

On land, there are valleys, cliffs, mountains and **plains**. Under the sea, there are similar features, but even bigger! These are shaped by many kinds of underwater forces.

At the edge of the sunlit continental shelf, the seabed goes down into the cold, dark depths.

In the shallows

Around the Earth's **continents** are shallow parts of the ocean known as continental shelves. The water here is usually less than 150 metres deep and the seabed is mostly flat. Some areas are covered by sand, silt and mud that is carried from the land by rivers. In other places, the tides and currents wash away the sand, leaving bare rocks and stones on the sea floor.

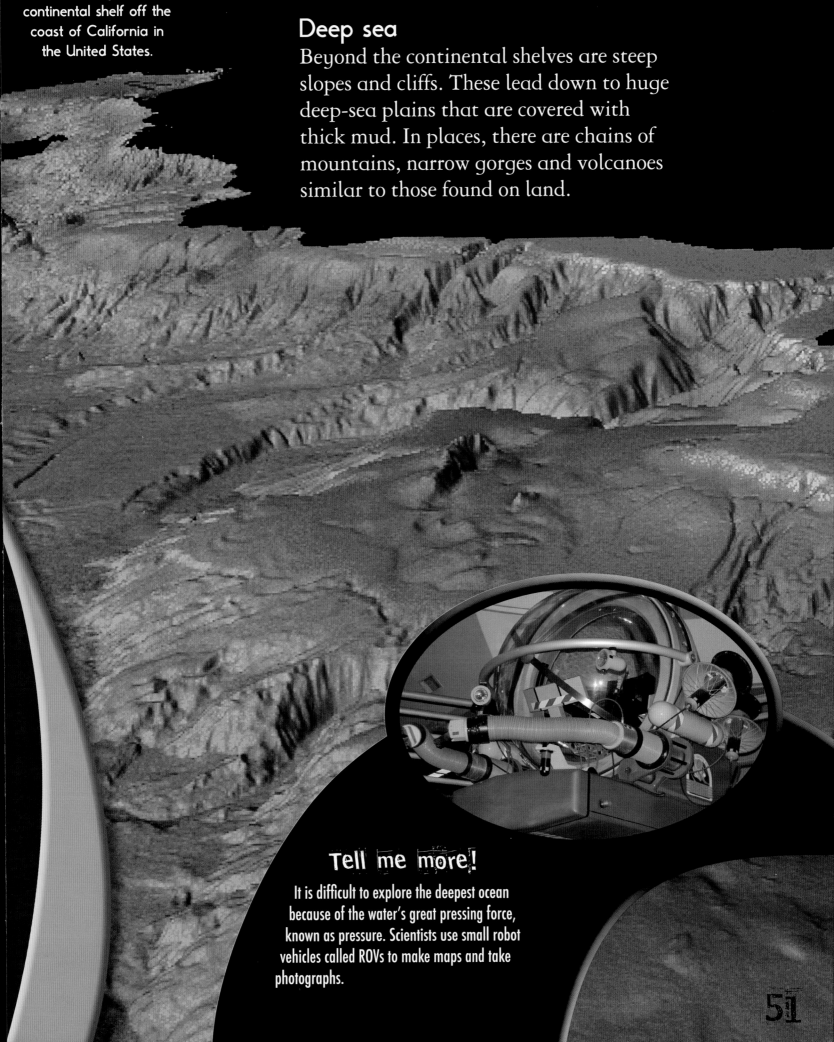

continental shelf off the coast of California in the United States.

Deep sea

Beyond the continental shelves are steep slopes and cliffs. These lead down to huge deep-sea plains that are covered with thick mud. In places, there are chains of mountains, narrow gorges and volcanoes similar to those found on land.

Tell me more!

It is difficult to explore the deepest ocean because of the water's great pressing force, known as pressure. Scientists use small robot vehicles called ROVs to make maps and take photographs.

51

Weather and life

The weather is different around the Earth. Hot or cold, dry or wet, it enables plants and animals to live in some places and not in others. Both weather and living things help to shape the Earth.

Lifeless regions
The coldest places on Earth are the polar regions in the far north and south, and the tops of mountains. Here it is too cold for living things to survive, and there are no plants to cover the land. The extreme weather on mountaintops, including rain, wind, snow and ice, wears away the rocks. They break into pieces that roll down the slopes.

Along a tropical shore, mangrove trees protect the land from waves.

Protected by plants

In **tropical** places on Earth, it is almost always warm all year around. If there is plenty of rain too, living things grow quickly. Rainforests cover some parts of the land in the tropics, and mangrove trees grow along the shores. These big, strong plants protect the soil and rocks from extreme weather, such as storms and floods.

Tree roots can force apart rocks and make cliffs collapse.

Severe weather erodes high mountains such as these, making them lower and rounder.

Seasonal changes

Between the tropics and the poles, most places have a warm summer and a cool winter. During summer, the Sun's heat makes cracks in rocks. In the cold winter, the rain and ice make the cracks wider. Over thousands of years, the rocks split apart. Even whole mountains wear down, and the shape of the landscape changes.

Tell me more!

When Mount Pinatubo in the Philippines erupted in 1991, dust darkened the skies for months. This made the weather cool and dull. Many plants, which had protected the land, died.

53

Animal action

Living things can have a big effect on the land's shape and its features. Even tiny bugs and worms can help to break up rocks and change the flow of rivers.

Roots and leaves

Plant roots stop sand and soil from being blown away. This allows bigger plants to take root and grow in the soil. When fallen leaves gather on the ground, they rot to make the soil richer and deeper.

Tiny workers

The small creatures that eat dead plants and animals, such as worms, slugs and insects, change the land. Their tunnels allow air and water into the soil so that more plants can grow into woods and forests.

Beavers changed the direction of this stream, which is now dry and rocky.

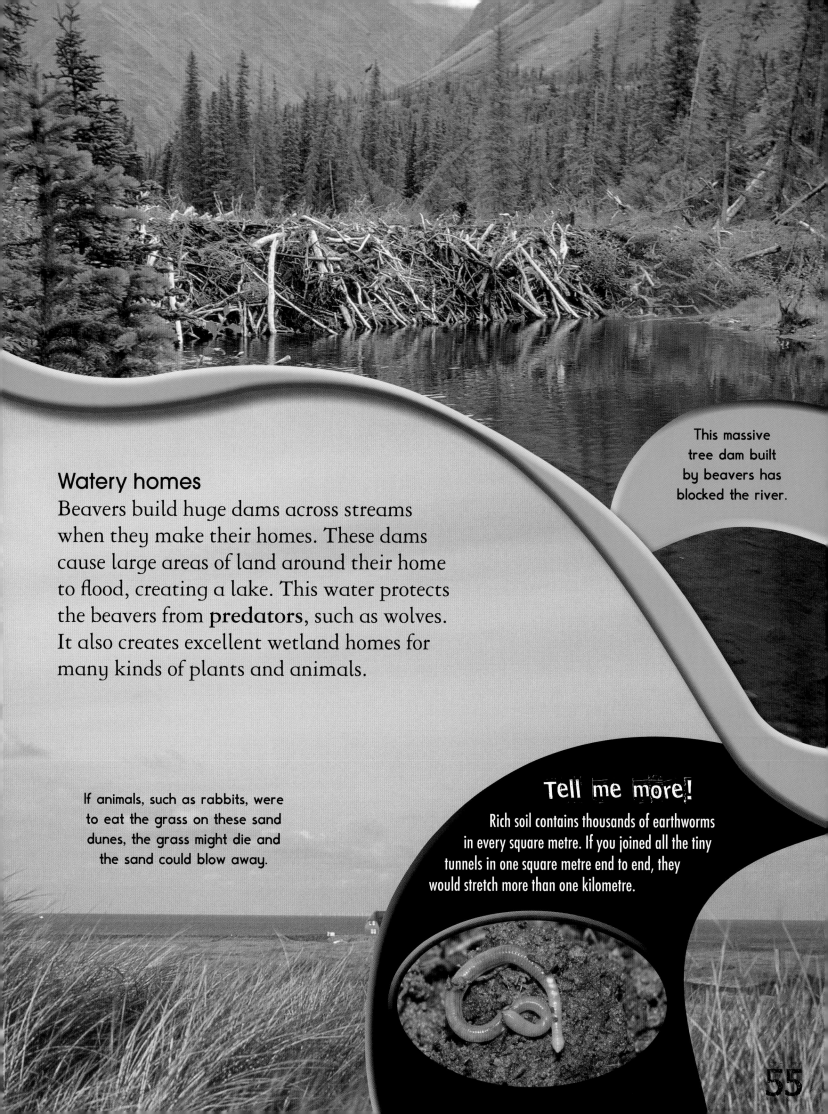

Watery homes

Beavers build huge dams across streams when they make their homes. These dams cause large areas of land around their home to flood, creating a lake. This water protects the beavers from **predators**, such as wolves. It also creates excellent wetland homes for many kinds of plants and animals.

This massive tree dam built by beavers has blocked the river.

If animals, such as rabbits, were to eat the grass on these sand dunes, the grass might die and the sand could blow away.

Tell me more!

Rich soil contains thousands of earthworms in every square metre. If you joined all the tiny tunnels in one square metre end to end, they would stretch more than one kilometre.

How we change the land

Long ago, people hardly changed the Earth at all. They hunted a few wild animals and gathered wild plants to eat. Today, the landscape is very different. Huge areas are covered with fields for farm animals and crops.

Farming the land

In the past, farms were built where trees and forests once grew. People cut down the trees and used the wood to make their farmhouses, their furniture and other useful things. Then they planted grass on the land for cows, sheep and other animals, and grew **crops**, such as wheat, barley and rice.

Tell me more!

Bad farming is reshaping huge areas that were once woodlands and grasslands. Every day around the world, an area the size of 10,000 football pitches is turning into dry, desert-like dust.

Losing forests

Changing land from forest to farmland can cause serious problems. This is because fields for crops and animals are not as good at soaking up heavy rain as forests. During a heavy downpour, rainwater washes away the useful soil from fields. This soil then clogs up ditches and rivers.

Flood waters from farm fields can wash into towns and cities.

Worn-out soil

Natural grasslands are much better than farmland at coping with a lack of water. During a long period without rain, called a drought, most farm crops die as they need a lot of water to grow. This leaves the soil without plant roots to hold it together, and it can blow away as dust.

Keeping too many farm animals may make the soil dry and thin.

Natural rainforests can soak up very heavy rain without causing floods.

Some trees lose their leaves in winter, which is good for the soil.

Human impact

When we build houses, shops, roads and parks, wild places have to be cleared. Sometimes, this can have a damaging effect on wildlife and on the natural **environment** in which we live.

Roads and buildings

The Earth is being shaped more and more by the people who live on it. New roads and buildings, for example, are using up more and more land. Sometimes, the way a river flows has to be changed to make way for a new town. This can cause the river to flood when there is heavy rain. Also, if people take out too much water from a river, it may dry up completely.

Heavy use of water has caused this river in China to dry up.

Around the world, there has been a surge in road building.

Tell me more!

One way to deal with the shortage of land for people to live on is to make new land. This has happened in the Netherlands, in northern Europe, where half of the land people live on has been reclaimed from the sea.

Chemical pollution

We change the Earth in ways we can't see. The chemicals we use every day can silently and invisibly pollute the air we breathe, the land in which we grow food and the water we drink. More and more, how we live, and the way in which we make things to use, is reshaping our world.

Every day, forests are cut down to make room for new towns.

Large cities can cause a lot of pollution in the air and in rivers.

These windmills were built on reclaimed land.

Tell me more!

This is molten lava. Lava is the molten
rock thrown up by a volcano during
an eruption and also the name for the
solid rock that forms when the molten
rock cools and hardens. Lava can reach
scorching temperatures of up to 1200°C!

Moving world

The Earth's surface is continually moving. Some changes are sudden, such as a volcanic eruption or an earthquake. Much bigger movements also happen, yet these are so slow we hardly notice.

Changing world

Over millions of years, the Earth's surface has changed many times. Rocks have been forced up to form mountains, which have then been worn away by wind and rain. Earthquakes have opened up huge cracks in the Earth's surface and hot volcanic material has covered vast areas of land.

Tell me more!

Nowhere on Earth is the land perfectly still. All land moves at least one centimetre per year, carrying rivers, valleys, hills and even towns and cities. Many places also move up or down at about the same rate.

All parts of a **tectonic plate** move, including the coastline. This area in Sognejord, Norway, has moved 25 kilometres west in the last 10,000 years.

Cracked surface

All of these changes happen because the Earth is not solid rock. Inside, it is partly melted. On the outside, the Earth is like a cracked egg, made of giant curved pieces called tectonic plates. The plates are pushed around by the swirling, partly melted rock beneath. These bump, rub and crash together.

Venezuela's Angel Falls is the world's highest waterfall, with a height of 979 metres. It formed when a huge chunk of rock slipped down.

63

Tectonic plates

The Earth's outer layer, the crust, is made of jagged-edged tectonic plates. These are constantly on the move, drifting on the part-liquid rock beneath.

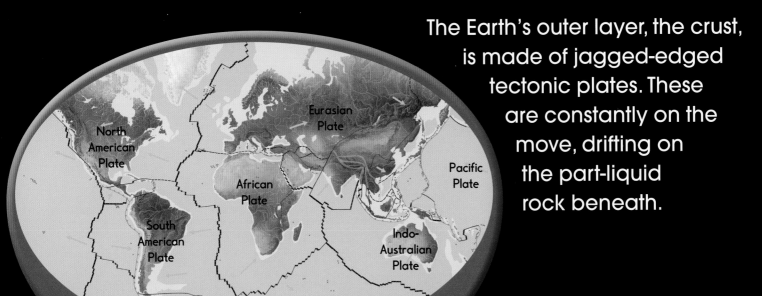

North American Plate

Eurasian Plate

African Plate

Pacific Plate

South American Plate

Indo-Australian Plate

Antarctic Plate

There are seven major tectonic plates and many smaller ones.

Subduction zone, where one plate slides under another

Building mountains

Under the Earth's crust is the partly melted mantle. This swirls and flows very slowly, carrying the plates along with it. In some places, the plates push against each other and their edges crumple to form mountains and valleys.

Sliding past

At a **transform fault**, two plates slide sideways past each other. This produces cracks in the ground and sometimes earthquakes. At the San Andreas Fault, which lies along the coast of western North America, the Pacific plate slides past the North American plate by more than one centimetre each year.

Tell me more!

The San Andreas Fault is 1300 kilometres long and varies in width from a few metres to hundreds of metres. There have been four big earthquakes along it in the past 150 years, and another is expected in the next 50 years.

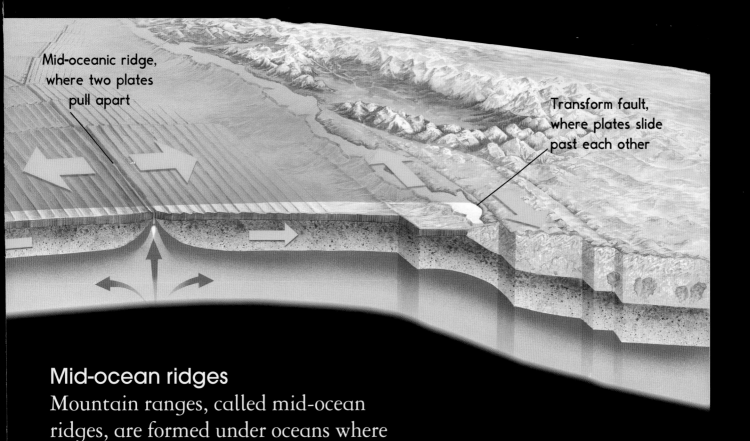

Mid-oceanic ridge, where two plates pull apart

Transform fault, where plates slide past each other

Mid-ocean ridges

Mountain ranges, called mid-ocean ridges, are formed under oceans where two tectonic plates move apart. When hot magma is forced up through the gap it hardens to form a ridge. The Mid-Atlantic Ridge is a mid-ocean ridge.

Pangaea

Around 200 million years ago, all land on Earth was joined together in one massive **supercontinent** we now call Pangaea.

Pangaea was surrounded by an enormous ocean known as Panthalassa.

One vast land

About 180 million years ago, Pangaea began to split apart. First it broke into two land masses, Laurasia in the north and Gondwana in the south. Then these split into the **continents** we know today. However, these took millions more years to drift to their present positions.

Tell me more!

Pangaea was not the first supercontinent. The Rodinia supercontinent lasted from 1100 to 750 million years ago. By 600 million years ago, the tectonic plates had changed again to form another supercontinent. This is known as Pannotia.

On the move

How do we know that the supercontinent we call Pangaea really existed? One way is to look at at map of the world to see how the continents may have once fitted together. The east coast of South America fits quite neatly with the west coast of Africa.

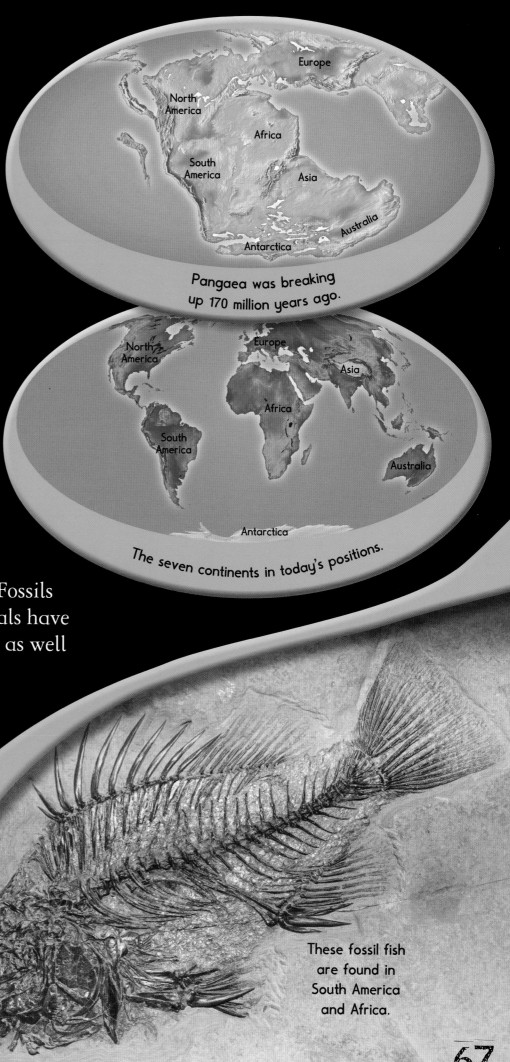

Pangaea was breaking up 170 million years ago.

The seven continents in today's positions.

Common fossils

There is also fossil evidence to show that the Pangaean supercontinent once existed. Fossils of the same plants and animals have been found in South America as well as in Africa. This indicates that these two continents were once linked together in one big landmass.

These fossil fish are found in South America and Africa.

Ring of Fire

All around the Pacific tectonic plate are earthquake and volcano zones. These make up the 'Ring of Fire'.

Mapping the plates

Scientists know that where the Earth's tectonic plates meet there are likely to be more earthquakes and volcanic eruptions. By keeping a careful record of all the earthquakes and eruptions that occur, they have been able to make a detailed map of the Earth's tectonic plates.

NORTH PACIFIC OCEAN

JAPAN

CHINA

PHILIPPINES

INDONESIA

AUSTRALIA

Tell me more!

As earthquakes are common in Japan, each month the country's schoolchildren take part in an earthquake drill. Those on lower floors of the school get under their desks and hold on tightly to the desk's legs. Children on upper floors practise using a chute to escape the building quickly.

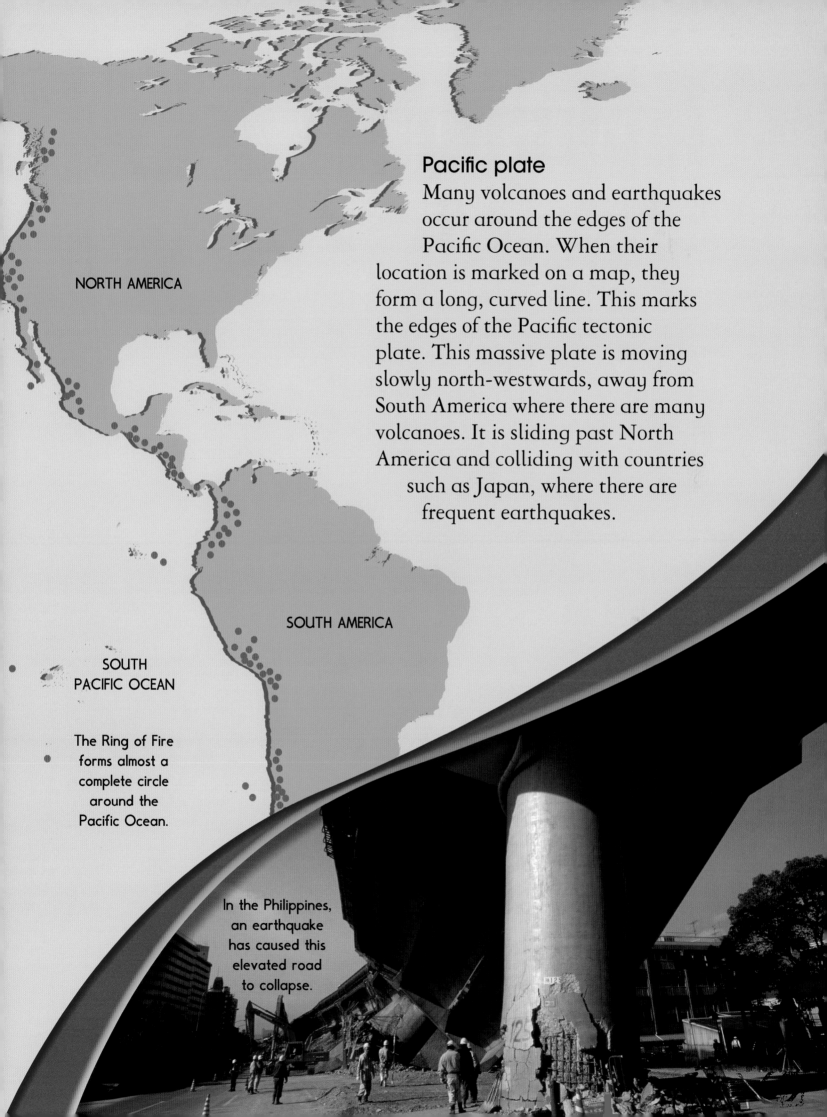

Pacific plate

Many volcanoes and earthquakes occur around the edges of the Pacific Ocean. When their location is marked on a map, they form a long, curved line. This marks the edges of the Pacific tectonic plate. This massive plate is moving slowly north-westwards, away from South America where there are many volcanoes. It is sliding past North America and colliding with countries such as Japan, where there are frequent earthquakes.

NORTH AMERICA

SOUTH AMERICA

SOUTH PACIFIC OCEAN

The Ring of Fire forms almost a complete circle around the Pacific Ocean.

In the Philippines, an earthquake has caused this elevated road to collapse.

Mountains

Mountains can be formed by volcanic activity as well as from movements in the tectonic plates.

Fold mountains

A type of mountain called a fold mountain is formed when tectonic plates squeeze against each other. When this happens, rock layers in the Earth's crust are pushed up, which causes them to fold and then crack. New fold mountains usually have sharp, jagged peaks.

The Himalayas began to form about 70 million years ago. They still rise by half a centimetre each year.

Edinburgh Castle in Scotland was built on a volcanic plug.

Volcanic plugs

Mountains are also formed from the remains of volcanoes. These mountains, which are called **volcanic plugs**, are made when magma fills up a volcano's vent and hardens into rock. After millions of years, the outer part of the volcano may be worn away, leaving the plug behind.

Tell me more!

The highest place on Earth is the top of Mount Everest, which is 8848 metres above sea level. The world's tallest mountain, however, is Mauna Kea in Hawaii, an extinct or dead volcano. Much of it is under water. Its total height from seabed to summit is about 9100 metres.

Dome mountains

Sometimes, huge blocks of rock in the Earth's crust are pushed up by the hot magma below. If the magma cannot find a way out through the crust, it may push up a weak part of the crust to form what is known as a dome mountain. This type of mountain, such as Half Dome mountain in California, often has a flattened top.

California's Half Dome mountain was formed flat on one side.

71

What is a volcano?

Volcanoes form when red-hot runny rock, called magma, pushes up from far below and out through the Earth's crust.

Volcanic mountain

A volcano is a place in the Earth's crust where material from deep inside the Earth forces its way out. Because this molten material is under immense pressure, it can also form a mountain. This happens when rock layers are pushed up by trapped magma, creating what is known as a volcanic mountain. When the volcano erupts, **lava** and ash from the volcano can add to the size of the volcanic mountain.

Lava from an erupting volcano flows down its slopes like a red-hot river of rock.

Tell me more!

Many people live close to active volcanoes. It sounds like a dangerous thing to do, but the soil around the volcano is often rich in minerals and good for growing crops.

Inside a volcano

When lava, ash and other materials shoot out of a volcano's crater, the volcano is said to be erupting. Before an eruption, hot magma rises through the Earth's mantle and collects in a large pool – the magma chamber. When the pressure here is great enough, magma is forced up a pipe called the conduit. It then bursts out as liquid rock called lava.

Gas and ash cloud

Vent

Lava

Crater

Conduit (pipe)

Magma chamber

Living with volcanoes

When there is a massive and unexpected volcanic eruption, the lives and safety of thousands of people may be at risk.

Extreme danger

The biggest danger for people from a volcanic eruption is not from falling rocks. Nor it is from the rivers of red-hot lava that travel downhill at speeds of up to 100 kilometres per hour. The greatest danger comes from poisonous clouds known as pyroclastic flows. These clouds can travel downhill at 700 kilometres per hour and may reach temperatures of 1000 degrees Celsius!

In 1980, the eruption of Mount St Helens in Washington state, USA, killed 57 people.

Tell me more!

One of the biggest eruptions in history was that of Mount Krakatau in Indonesia. In 1883, the whole volcanic island blew apart. More than 35,000 people died in the explosion and from the giant waves, or **tsunamis**, that it caused.

Seeking safety

Today, scientists can sometimes warn people living near an active volcano that it is about to erupt, so that they can quickly move to safe areas. The signs they look for include small earthquakes, the ground around a volcano becoming hot and **tremors** in the ground.

Deadly clouds

Anyone unlucky enough to be caught up in a pyroclastic flow would probably be killed instantly. This happened in the town of Pompeii in Italy. In 79 AD, Mount Vesuvius erupted and covered the entire town and its doomed inhabitants in deadly volcanic ash. The town, which was completely covered, lay hidden for almost 1600 years.

A plaster cast of a victim of the tragedy in Pompeii.

Super-volcanoes

Super-volcanoes are giant volcanoes covering vast areas.
If one were to erupt, it could endanger all life on Earth.

Massive destruction

A super-volcano forms where magma tries to force its way up through the crust but cannot break through. If this were to happen, more and more pressure would build up over a wider and wider area. At some point, perhaps, half a continent may explode! The last super-volcano eruption took place many thousands of years ago.

Warning signs

When large pools of magma collect deep down, hot springs and geysers may appear on the Earth's surface. These features could show that a super-volcano is building up beneath.

White Dome Geyser, in Yellowstone National Park, USA, gushes out a hot spray up to 9 metres high.

Tell me more!

Earth is not the only planet to have super-volcanoes. They have been spotted on some of the moons of Jupiter and Saturn.

A super-volcano on Io, a moon of Jupiter.

Scientists do not know when the next devastating super-volcanic eruption will take place.

The Siberian Traps, Russia

Yellowstone, Wyoming

Long Valley Caldera, California

Valles Calderas, New Mexico

Kyushu, Southern Japan

Aira Caldera, Kagoshima

Taupo Volcano, New Zealand

Scientists believe that there are seven sites around the world that could become super-volcanoes in the future.

World event

If a super-volcano were to erupt, huge areas of Earth would be covered with lava and ash. The effects would be felt all around the world and could last for many years. The Lake Toba super-volcano in Sumatra, Indonesia, exploded about 75,000 years ago. Temperatures around the world dropped, and more than half the people in the world died.

Undersea volcanoes

As well as the volcanoes on land, there are many more deep under the sea.

Rock shapes

Undersea volcanoes are similar to those on land. They occur along the edges of tectonic plates and they erupt lava, ash and gases. Lava cools very quickly in sea water, forming strange rock shapes on the seabed.

Undersea lava hardens as bulges called pillow lava.

Strange crabs, fish and worms live around deep-sea hydrothermal vents

Black smokers

A hydrothermal vent is a crack in the Earth's crust through which very hot water escapes. This water can be as hot as 400 degrees Celsius. On land, these cracks form geysers and hot water springs. On the ocean floor, hydrothermal vents can become chimney-like structures known as black smokers. The hot water they spew out is rich in minerals, which form millions of tiny particles. As they cool down in the sea water, the particles produce dark clouds.

Black smokers are found on the seabed in all oceans, especially the Atlantic Ocean.

Tell me more!

The Earth's crust is much thinner on the sea bed than on the land. So more volcanoes occur underwater than on the continents. More than three-quarters of all lava rock forms under the oceans.

Earthquakes

Earthquakes can occur anywhere on Earth. The worst, however, usually strike parts of the world where the tectonic plates meet.

Violent movements

The worst earthquakes happen when the sideways pressure between two tectonic plates builds up so much that they move suddenly and violently. The centre of an earthquake is usually deep underground. The place above it on the surface, where it is felt most violently, is the **epicentre**.

Plates slip sideways

Epicentre

Shock waves spread out

Centre

A sudden sideways movement of tectonic plates can cause earthquakes.

Some 4600 people lost their lives as a result of the 1995 earthquake that rocked Kobe in Japan.

Plenty of warning

Many of the worst earthquakes have been unexpected. The city of San Francisco in California, in the United States, has been hit by several major earthquakes in the past. Today, scientists in this region measure what is happening deep underground to give people plenty of warning of a possible earthquake.

In 1906, San Francisco, California, USA, was devastated by a massive earthquake.

Tell me more!

Every day, there are about 3000 earthquakes on Earth. Most of these are so small that no one realises that they have actually happened!

Landslides

The landscape can change when parts of mountains or cliffs fall to the land or the sea below. These are known as landslides or landslips.

Whole hillsides can slide away.

Causes of landslides

Landslides can be caused by earthquakes, by underground water during wet weather or by the wearing away of land to leave overhanging rocks. Landslides also happen when too many trees on hills and mountains are cut down. This can cause an entire side of a hill or mountain to slip down.

Deadly mudslides

When soil is very wet, it turns into mud. This is when a mudslide can strike. Mudslides, which can also carry tonnes of rocks, may reach speeds of 80 kilometres per hour. Because mudslides are unpredictable, they can be extremely dangerous.

Danger to life

An avalanche is a mass of snow that rushes down a mountainside. It can destroy buildings that lie in its path. Avalanches often start after heavy winter snow. They can be triggered by a simple human activity, such as snowboarding, or by natural events, such as high winds. In mountain regions, avalanches pose the greatest danger to human life.

In 2002, a huge 30-kilometre landslide in the Koban Valley, Russia, killed 125 people.

Avalanches travel faster than people can run, or even ski.

Tell me more!

Landslides into the sea can cause tsunamis. Some scientists think that a volcanic eruption could start a massive landslide in the Canary Islands, which may then create a huge tsunami. This giant wave could rush across the Atlantic Ocean and devastate the east coast of America.

Tsunamis

A tsunami is a giant wave that rushes up from the sea and onto the land. The massive wall of water can destroy anything that lies in its path.

What causes tsunamis?

A tsunami may be triggered by a violent earthquake that pushes up the seabed. It can also be caused by an underwater volcano or even by a huge landslide into the sea.

Undersea earthquake

Low, fast surface waves

Even a small tsunami can wash away cars and break up roads.

Wall of water

A tsunami usually starts deep in the ocean. At first, it looks like an ordinary wave on the ocean's surface. People on ships far out at sea do not even notice that something is happening. At this point, the tsunami is moving very fast. As the sea becomes shallower around the coast, the tsunami slows down and becomes much higher.

The 2004 Indian Ocean tsunami killed more than 220,000 people.

Wave builds higher

Wave slows down

Wave breaks onto shore

Hitting the shore

Tsunamis can rise to the height of a two-storey building just before they hit the shore. When a tsunami finally breaks, the force of the water is so strong it destroys buildings and can move heavy objects far inland.

A tsunami may travel many hundreds of kilometres at sea before it crashes onto the shore.

Tell me more!

Can animals tell that a tsunami is going to happen before we can? Just before the 2004 Indian Ocean tsunami, people saw animals behaving oddly. Elephants rushed to higher ground and dogs refused to go on the beach. d that they heard the Tsunami coming.

When the Earth shakes

The biggest movements on Earth happen when giant rocks from space, such as **asteroids**, **meteorites** and comets, smash into the planet.

Sudden impact

About every 10 million years, on average, a massive chunk of rock more than five kilometres across hurtles from space into the Earth. What happens depends on how fast it travels, the angle at which it strikes, and where it hits – in the mountains, on a tectonic plate edge or in the sea.

Tell me more!

A meteorite impact 65 million years ago may have wiped out the dinosaurs. Scientists have discovered the remains of an 180-metre wide crater on the coast of Mexico. This crater, called Chicxulub, may mark the site where the meteorite struck.

Earth on the move

A big impact sets off many natural disasters. Stuck tectonic plates slip, triggering massive earthquakes. The cracked crust allows more volcanoes to erupt, and even super-volcanoes. Huge tsunamis crash onto shores around the world. The whole Earth seems on the move.

Almost 65 million years ago, dinosaurs and **pterosaurs** flee the giant meteorite that will wipe them out and ravage the whole Earth.

Future strike

Great impacts are becoming rarer as many of the big space rocks in the Solar System have already crashed into other planets or their moons. From what we know, Earth's next big collision could be in 800 years – and even that is unlikely.

At 1200 metres across, Barringer Crater, in Arizona, USA, was formed by a 50-metre meteorite 40,000 years ago.

87

Tell me more!

This is a cyclone over the Pacific Ocean.
A cyclone is a violent tropical storm. They
are accompanied by torrential rain and very
strong winds that usually spiral in a circle.
Some cyclones cover areas of 200 kilometers!

Climate or weather?

Weather is what happens over hours and days. It can change very quickly. Climate, on the other hand, may not change for thousands of years.

Changing weather

Weather occurs over a short period of time — sometimes just for a few minutes! In some places, it is easy to predict. In a tropical desert, for example, it is likely to be hot and dry, day after day. But in another place, the weather can be much more varied. Most summer days are warm, but any one day may be sunny or cloudy, wet or dry.

This river in Saskatoon, Canada, regularly freezes in winter.

The Sun is shining, but the rainbow tells us that there is rain nearby.

Different climates

The climate is the general type of weather over many years and centuries. In each place, we know what to expect from the climate. Northern Canada has bitterly cold winters with lots of snow. India has heavy rain towards the end of the summer.

Tell me more!

Over millions of years, the Earth has had many Ice Ages. About 20,000 years ago, most of Europe and North America was covered with ice. This Ice Age came to an end around 10,000 years ago.

A tropical climate is warm all year around, year after year.

Sun, rain and wind

Our weather is marked by many different features. Temperatures can be freezing cold or baking hot, while rain may start as a light drizzle and become a heavy downpour. Winds can change from a calm breeze to a howling hurricane, and bright sunshine can suddenly be blotted out by dark rain clouds.

Why does weather happen?

The heat of the Sun and the spinning of the world are the most important factors that create weather on Earth.

Our atmosphere

The Earth's **atmosphere** is made up of a layer of gases that surrounds our planet. The atmosphere contains the **oxygen** we need to breathe and protects us from the Sun's dangerous rays. The heat of the Sun and the turning of the Earth make the atmosphere move all the time. It is this movement that gives us our weather.

Wind is the air of the atmosphere moving sideways from one place to another.

Moving air

As the Earth turns, the Sun heats the gases, or air, of the atmosphere by different amounts. As air gets warmer, it rises, and cooler air flows from somewhere else to take its place. This flow or current of air creates winds that vary in strength and direction.

Tell me more!

High above the surface of the Earth there are very fast winds known as **jet streams**. Aircraft pilots make use of these speedy jet streams to fly more quickly from one place to another.

Cloudy skies

The Sun's energy heats up sea water, too. As the sea warms, tiny drops of water become **water vapour** and rise into the atmosphere. This water vapour forms clouds, which are moved by air currents. When the clouds cool, the water vapour turns into water and we get rain.

Clouds often form over the ocean and are blown by air currents.

Hottest and coldest

The farther you go from the middle of the Earth towards its top or bottom, and the higher you are, the colder it becomes.

The Sun's warmth heats the Earth's middle most.

Heat from the Sun

The Equator is an imaginary line around the Earth, midway between the North Pole and the South Pole. On either side of the Equator is the region called the tropics. Here the Sun is high in the sky, so it is hot all year around. Nearer the poles, the Sun is low in the sky and has much less warming power.

Even though Mount Kilimanjaro is in the tropics, its peak is so high that it is often covered with snow.

High altitudes

There is another reason why some places are very cold. This reason is their height above sea level, which is known as altitude. Tibet, which has some of the world's tallest mountains, is a cold country. Africa's famous Mount Kilimanjaro is almost on the Equator, and yet the top is covered in snow!

Tell me more!

The coldest place on Earth is Antarctica. The lowest temperature ever recorded here was minus 89 degrees Celsius. The hottest ever temperature, 58 degrees Celsius, was recorded in Libya in North Africa.

Land temperatures

Places in the middle of Earth's continents have extreme temperatures. They can be very cold in winter and very hot in summer. This is because the land warms up more quickly than the sea, but also loses its heat more quickly. Sea currents also affect temperatures on land. Western Europe has a mild climate because of a warm water current called the Gulf Stream that flows up from the hot tropics.

Norway is in the far north of Europe and so has much snow and ice in winter.

Seasons

Seasonal changes, which are caused by the Sun, affect many living things on Earth.

Summer

Spring

Autumn

Winter

Four seasons

Between the poles and the tropics are the **temperate lands**. Most of these have four seasons – warm summer, cool autumn, cold winter and warming up again in spring. In tropical places it's warm all year, but there is usually a wet and a dry season.

Spring to life

All living things adapt to temperature changes and the amount of daylight they get. Trees in temperate areas are usually deciduous – they lose their leaves in the winter. Here, also, animals may **hibernate** in winter and seeds will not start to grow until spring.

This photograph was taken several times in one winter's day in the far north. It shows how the Sun rises only a short way above the horizon and soon sets, giving just a few hours of daylight.

Why do we get seasons?

The Earth is tilted as it moves around the Sun once each year. For part of the year, the northern half is closer to the Sun, giving summer here. For the other part of the year, the Earth's southern half is nearer and has its summer. Countries near the poles have just a few hours of winter daylight. On the Equator, day and night are the same all year around.

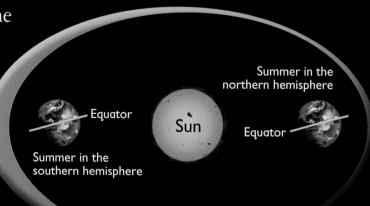

Summer in the northern hemisphere

Equator

Sun

Equator

Summer in the southern hemisphere

Rain cycle

Water is always moving around and around in a cycle between the surface of the Earth and the sky.

Cloud formation

The Sun's heat warms surface water in oceans, lakes and rivers. This causes water vapour to form through a process known as **evaporation**. As the water vapour rises in the air, it passes through cooler air, which turns the water vapour into millions and millions of drops of water. It is these drops that form clouds.

Heavy clouds gather over the land. In the distance, rain is falling.

Back to the ocean

When water drops in a cloud become too heavy, they fall as rain. If air temperatures are low, these water drops freeze into tiny crystals and turn into snow. After falling, rain finds its way back to the ocean in streams and rivers. In other words, the water goes back to where it came from, ready for the rain cycle to begin all over again.

Ontario, Canada, in the grip of winter snow.

Clouds form in the cool air

Rain falls and water flows along streams and rivers back to the ocean

Water evaporates from the ocean

99

Water of life

Lack of rain and over-use of water are turning this Chinese forest into a desert.

Nothing can live without water. But too much water, or too little, can greatly harm people, farm animals, crops and wildlife.

Lack of water

In some parts of the world, such as deserts, it is normal for only a small amount of rain to fall each year. Droughts, however, happen in places where rain does usually fall each year. If the rains don't arrive, then crops may fail and animals may die. When droughts last for several years, all plants die. The soil dries out, turns to dust and blows away.

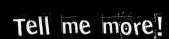

Tell me more!

The spadefoot toad, which lives in the Sonoran Desert in North America, is perfectly adapted to cope with drought. This toad can stay in its burrow without eating or drinking for nine months!

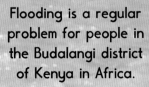

Flooding is a regular problem for people in the Budalangi district of Kenya in Africa.

Too much water

Severe problems can also occur when more than a normal amount of rain falls in a year or over a short period of time. When this happens, the soil cannot soak up the extra water in the usual way. Rivers may burst their banks and flood homes, roads and farmland.

Stormy weather

A storm usually brings dark clouds, strong winds, rain and sometimes thunder and lightning. These are caused by the Sun's heat quickly warming parts of the atmosphere.

Wind and rain

Winds are made up of air that is moving from places where it has a higher pressure to areas of lower pressure. The more difference there is in air pressure, the faster the wind moves. Winds faster than 90 kilometres per hour are called a storm. If warm, damp air meets cold air here, the water vapour turns to rain, which can be very heavy and cause floods.

Hot air rising from this desert has triggered a thunderstorm.

Tell me more!

Lightning flashes move at up to 1000 kilometres per second. They can be as hot as 30,000 degrees Celsius – five times hotter than the surface of the Sun!

Thunder and lightning

When raindrops rub against each other in a cloud they create electricity. This electricity causes giant sparks to jump from one part of the cloud to another, or to shoot down to the ground. This is lightning. Since lightning is extremely hot, it heats up the air around, which expands and forms giant **sound waves**. These waves produce the massive booming sound we call thunder.

This tree in the Ligurian Alps in Italy has been destroyed by lightning.

Hurricanes

The swirling storms known as hurricanes occur every year. When these ferocious winds strike land, they can cause immense amounts of damage and injury.

The strongest **cyclone** to hit Australia in 2006 was called Cyclone Monica.

Terrible damage
A hurricane is a violent tropical storm that forms over warm ocean waters near to the Equator. When a hurricane hits land, it can cause terrible damage. Many people may be injured, or even die.

What causes hurricanes?

Hurricanes form in the summer months. Under the Sun's heat, water vapour rises from the ocean's surface. When the vapour reaches the top of the clouds, it cools and sinks, producing heavy rain. Air currents and the spinning of the Earth then set the storm clouds spinning faster and faster. This forms a typical tropical hurricane.

Winds move outwards

Cold air sinks

Warm air rises

A hurricane forms over the ocean.

A violent hurricane hits land in the tropics.

Tell me more!

New Orleans, Louisiana, USA, was flooded by Hurricane Katrina in 2005. More than 1800 people lost their lives in the tragedy.

Tornadoes

Tornadoes generate some of the fastest winds on the planet. These winds can reach speeds of up to 400 kilometres per hour.

Hot air rising ——

Vortex ——

High winds

Tornadoes are formed inside thunderclouds. A column of rising hot air is set spinning by two air currents moving in opposite directions. This spinning column of air is called a vortex. If the vortex reaches the ground, a tornado is formed. Dust and solid objects will then be sucked up by the tornado, causing serious damage. The high winds around the base of the vortex also cause huge destruction.

A tornado rips across the Texas landscape in the United States.

Spring and summer

Tornadoes are found across the world. Although they can occur at any time of the year, most strike during the spring and early summer. Some of the most severe tornadoes happen in the United States, India and Bangladesh.

Tell me more!

People living in areas where there are severe tornadoes sometimes build a safe room in their house called an in-house shelter. This may be a cupboard or a bathroom. It usually has no windows and a strong door and walls made of steel.

A tornado tore apart these houses in Iowa, which is part of the region called 'Tornado Alley' in the United States.

Five horses

Tornadoes suck up and move heavy objects, including living creatures! In 1990, a tornado in Illinois , USA, picked up a 20-tonne lorry and moved it 350 metres. In Kansas in 1915, five horses were lifted up by a tornado and carried for half a kilometre. The horses were found alive, if not very happy!

Forecasting

Weather scientists are known as meteorologists. They have many gadgets to help them predict or forecast the weather around the world.

Highs and lows
Changes in air pressure are very important in forecasting. High pressure usually means calm weather, with warm sunshine in summer and cold, sunny days in winter. Low pressure brings wind, cloud and rain.

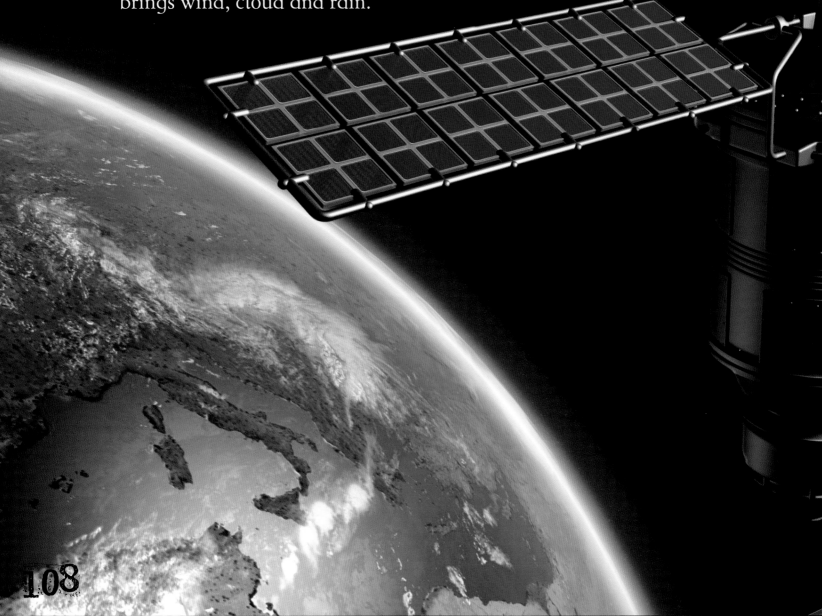

Weather stations

To help them predict the weather, meteorologists collect and process information from weather stations all around the world. This information includes differences in air pressure as well as temperature, rainfall and wind speeds.

Tell me more!

Meteorologists use some of the world's most powerful computers, known as **supercomputers**, to deal with the huge amounts of information that come from satellites and weather stations.

Using satellites

Information from satellites has made weather forecasting more accurate. Photographs can show clouds forming and moving. Satellites also measure temperatures on the surface of the Earth and at the tops of clouds.

Weather satellites beam down information about air pressure, temperature, clouds and winds to weather centres on the ground.

Anemometer for wind speed

A typical small weather station.

Solar panel measures the Sun's light and heat

Wind vane shows wind direction

Barometer for air pressure

Hygrometer for humidity (water vapour content)

Thermometer for temperature

109

Weather warning

People need to know about severe weather,
such as hurricanes, snowstorms and tornadoes,
so they can prepare and stay safe.

Predicting weather

The local weather helps to predict what the
next few hours or days will bring. Wind
direction, the types of clouds and temperature
changes all suggest what is coming. But the
bigger the area, the more complicated it gets.

A meteorologist tracking a
hurricane on his computer.

Tracking hurricanes

People who live in a hurricane
area look at the weather
warnings as one of these violent
storms approaches. Forecasters
track the hurricane far out at
sea and try to predict when and
where it might strike land, and
how severe it will be.

Sounding the alarm

Predicting tornadoes is more difficult because they happen without warning. With the help of **radar**, meteorologists can locate tornadoes and **sirens** are used to warn people in danger.

Tell me more!

The Sun looks red in the morning and evening because of its low position in the sky. A red Sun in the morning can mean that rain is on the way. A red Sun in the evening, however, usually indicates that dry weather is coming!

Photographs from space, such as this of hurricane Katrina in 2005, help predict weather.

Harvest time

Farmers rely on dry weather to gather in ripe crops. An urgent weather warning means they can speed up the harvest before storms ruin the crops.

This harvester gets to work before rain comes.

Climate change

When we burn fuel in homes, vehicles, factories and power stations, we make greenhouse gases that can cause climate change.

In some areas, climate change may mean that no rain fails, leading to drought.

Constant change

Scientists believe that climate change is not new – the Earth's climate has changed many times. When the dinosaurs walked the Earth, the world was very much warmer than it is today. During the Ice Age, when much of the Earth was covered with ice, it was very much colder!

Greenhouse gases

Today, human activities are releasing large amounts of damaging gases into the atmosphere. These gases, such as carbon dioxide and methane, are known as greenhouse gases. Like a greenhouse, they stop heat escaping. Scientists believe that this is making the Earth warm up faster than it should.

Greenhouse gases stop warmth escaping from the atmosphere.

Less heat escapes into space

Atmosphere

Greenhouse gases trap more heat

Earth's surface

In other areas, climate change may lead to heavy rain and floods.

Tell me more!

Today, around 1500 people live in the Tokelau islands in the South Pacific Ocean. These islands rise no more than two metres above sea level. If global warming causes sea levels to rise, the Tokelau islands could disappear altogether under water.

Floods and droughts

A warming world could have devastating consequences for many people. Firstly, as the world's ice melts, sea levels will rise. This will flood low-lying land with salt water. There may also be more storms and droughts as the climate changes, making it difficult to live in some parts of the world.

The low-lying Maldive Islands in the Indian Ocean are threatened by rising seas.

Green energy

To slow the rate of climate change we must use less energy. We also need to generate energy in ways that do not produce damaging carbon dioxide and other greenhouse gases.

Saving energy

Much of the energy we use in our homes and factories is wasted. We can reduce this waste by using equipment that requires less electricity to work, such as low-energy lightbulbs. We can also **insulate** buildings so that much less heat is lost through the walls and roofs.

Tell me more!

The sea itself can be a source of energy. Engineers are finding ways to turn the power of waves and tides into electricity.

Electricity-generating turbines at sea are sometimes grouped together as a wind farm.

Wind power

Wind can be a problem – but it can be helpful too! **Wind turbines** generate electricity without producing greenhouse gases. Many wind turbines are set up out at sea. It is more expensive to build these offshore, but the wind blows more steadily out at sea.

Solar energy

The Sun's energy, called solar energy, powers our weather and climate. We can turn sunlight into electricity by using devices called photovoltaic cells, which are mounted on solar panels. The Sun's warmth can also be used to heat water for homes and factories.

A solar power station at Sanlucar in Spain.

115

Glossary

Asteroid Huge lump of space rock many kilometres wide, going around the Sun.

Atmosphere The layer of gases around the Earth.

Carbon Natural substance that forms coal and diamonds and is found in many kinds of rock.

Comet Big ball of ice and dust going around the Sun.

Compass Long, slim magnetised needle that points north–south.

Continent Very large area, or mass, of land.

Crops Plants grown by people for food or products.

Crust Hard, rocky outermost layer of the Earth.

Cyclone Strong, swirling winds that can develop into a hurricane-like storm.

Delta Area of flat land near the coast where a river splits into many channels.

Dissolve Tiny particles spread out in a liquid.

Environment The surroundings, including rocks, soil, plants, animals and the weather.

Epicentre Place on the earth's surface above the centre of an earthquake, where it is felt most strongly.

Eruption When liquid rock from deep in the Earth comes up through the crust.

Evaporation The process of changing a liquid into gas.

Expansion Getting bigger when heated or when frozen.

Fjord Deep-sea inlet created by a glacier.

Flood plain Area of land by a river that is regularly flooded.

Fossil Remains of a living thing preserved in rocks.

Glacier Huge river of ice sliding downhill.

Geyser A spring that erupts hot water and steam, caused by a magma pool close to the surface.

Gorge Deep valley cut by a river.

Gravity Force that pulls objects towards each other.

Hibernate Sleep through the winter when food is difficult to find.

Ice Age Period of time when the Earth was much colder and large areas were covered with ice.

Igneous rock Rock formed when melted lava or magma cools and hardens.

Insulate Prevent heat or cold from being lost.

Jet stream Strong, steady winds, which are very high in the atmosphere.

Lava When magma erupts from a volcano, it is known as lava.

Magma Hot, semi-liquid rock that makes up the Earth's outer core.

Mammoth Huge elephant-like creature which is now extinct (has died out).

Mantle A layer between the Earth's crust and its core.

Metamorphic rock Rock that is changed by great heat and pressure, but without melting.

Meteorite Large lump of rock travelling through space.

Mineral Natural substance that makes up rocks.

Natural gas Gas found in the Earth's crust that we burn as fuel.

Oxygen Gas that animals and plants need to stay alive.

Plain Flat area, usually covered by grass or similar low plants.

Plankton Tiny plants and animals floating in seas and big lakes.

Plate Section of the Earth's surface that floats on the liquid, or molten, rock beneath it.

Polar regions Very cold areas around the North and South Poles.

Predator Animal that kills other animals for food.

Pressure Pressing or pushing force.

Pterosaurs Flying creatures that thrived during the Age of Dinosaurs but are now all extinct.

Radar Device that uses radio waves to detect objects

Radioactive substance Substance that gives off rays, which can harm living things.

ROVs Remotely operated underwater vehicles.

Sauropod Group of very big dinosaurs with a small head, long neck and tail, huge body and four straight legs.

Sediment Tiny bits or particles that settle into layers.

Sedimentary rock Rock formed by squeezing together particles of sediments.

Silt Very small or fine particles of sediments, like slippery mud.

Sinkhole Deep hole at the surface into which water flows underground.

Siren Device that makes a very loud noise, usually as a warning.

Sound waves Vibrations that carry sound.

Subduction zone Area where one tectonic plate is pushed down under the edge of another.

Supercomputer Computer that is millions of times faster and more powerful than an ordinary home computer.

Supercontinent Vast area of land made of two or more continents connected together.

Supernova A massive exploding star.

Swamp Place with both ground and water, often lots of muddy pools and soft, wet soil.

Tectonic plate Large curved section of the Earth's outer layer, the crust.

Temperate lands The parts of the Earth that have mild changes in weather between summer and winter.

Trace A sign, or tiny remains of an animal or plant that died long ago.

Transform fault Area where one tectonic plate slides past another.

Tremor Shaking or vibrations.

Tropical Always-warm places situated on either side of the Equator, around the middle of the Earth.

Tsunami Massive, powerful wave set off by an earthquake, volcano or landslip.

Volcanic plug Central part of a volcano, where the lava has gone very hard.

Water vapour Water in the form of an invisible gas that floats in air.

Wetland Place with large amounts of water, such as a river, lake, marsh or swamp.

Wind turbine Tall tower with spinning blades that makes electricity from wind energy.

Index

Ideas for parents and teachers

Here are some practical activities that children can do at school or at home.

Edible Earth
Use a glass tumbler to build up, in layers, a cross-section of the Earth. Make the hard inner core from toffee and the outer core from jelly. Use a mixture of crispy cereal and marshmallow for the mantle. Make the crust from chocolate, complete with mountains! If hot ingredients are used, children should be supervised.

Create a compass
To make a working compass you will need a sewing needle, a magnet, a small circular piece of cork or plastic and a dish of water.
• Magnetise the needle by stroking it with the magnet in the same direction 30 times.
• Rest the needle on top of the cork and float the cork on the water. Slowly, the needle will turn to point north and south.

Fossils in walls
Look for traces of fossils in the walls of buildings made from limestone. Use thin white paper and crayons to make rubbings of any fossils found.

Geology museum
Start collecting rocks, minerals and fossils. Many samples are inexpensive to buy from specialist shops, or can be collected for free. Caution: some sites strictly forbid visitors from collecting samples.

Simulate an earthquake
You will need some stiff cardboard, a flat tray and some play sand.
• Place two pieces of cardboard side by side on the tray.
• Cover the cardboard with slightly damp sand. Pat the sand down firmly.
• Slide the cards against each other, or pull them apart, to simulate the effects of an earthquake on the Earth's surface. The two pieces of cardboard represent adjacent tectonic plates.

Earthquake information
Design a poster informing people what they should do in the event of an earthquake or a tsunami alert.

Glossary games
Provide a dozen small cards, which should be about 6 centimetres by 3 centimetres. Six cards should be in one colour, and six in another colour.
• Select a dozen of the terms defined in this book's glossary on page 116.
• Using a set of cards in one colour, write a glossary term on each card.
• On the cards of the other colour, copy the glossary definitions of the chosen words.

The cards can be used to play various games.
• Match cards with their definitions.
• Select a word card and define the term.
• Pick a definition card and guess the term.
• Spread all the cards on the table so that the writing can't be seen. Turn over two cards. If the word and definition match, remove these cards and carry on. If they don't, turn the cards over again and select two other cards.

Keeping a weather diary
For this project you will need a diary, or a notebook or loose-leaf folder. Children can keep a daily record of the weather in the local area. Alternatively, they could record worldwide extreme weather events and locations, including hurricanes, torrential rain, prolonged freezing weather and so on. The National Oceanic and Atmospheric Administration website is a good source of information about weather events around the world (www.noaa.gov/)*.

* Website information is correct at time of going to press. The publishers are not responsible for any content found on internet sites, or third-party websites.